Scientists
IN ACTION

BIOLOGISTS
IN ACTION

CRABTREE
PUBLISHING COMPANY
WWW.CRABTREEBOOKS.COM

Anne Rooney

Author: Anne Rooney

Series research and development: Reagan Miller

Editorial director: Kathy Middleton

Photo research: James Nixon

Editors: Paul Humphrey, James Nixon, Ellen Rodger

Proofreader: Lorna Notsch

Designer: Keith Williams (sprout.uk.com)

Prepress technician: Samara Parent

Print coordinator: Katherine Berti

Layout: Keith Williams (sprout.uk.com)

Consultant: Brianne Manning

Produced for Crabtree Publishing Company
by Discovery Books

Cover image: A biologist analyzes a water sample

Photographs:

Alamy: pp. 4 (Minden Pictures), 5 (Media Drum World), 7 bottom (BSIP SA), 10 (Minden Pictures), 11 top (Douglas R. Clifford/Tampa Bay Times via ZUMA Wire), 13 top (Minden Pictures) 14 (Suzanne Long), 17 top (Minden Pictures), 17 bottom (Olaf Doering), 18 (Robbie Shone), 20 top (Frans Lanting Studio), 20 bottom (Minden Pictures), 24 top (Natural History Collection).

Jane Weinstock: p. 19 top.

Shutterstock: pp. 6 (Francescomoufotografo), 8 left (Dennis Jacobsen), 8 right (NOOR RADYA BINTI MD RADZI), 9 bottom (Matej Kastelic), 11 bottom (Kristel Segeren), 12 (Joanne Weston), 15 top (Abd. Halim Hadi), 15 bottom (Byelikova Oksana), 16 (FrameStockFootages), 19 bottom (Nestor Rizhniak), 21 (Gorodenkoff), 22 (Dan Logan), 23 top (Igor Banaszczyk), 25 (Rich Carey), 26 top (Muellek Josef), 26 bottom (Dmitry Naumov), 27 top (Lapina), 27 bottom (Satirus), 28 (Africa Studio), 29 top (Elizaveta Galitckaia), 29 bottom (ruigsantos).

Wikimedia: pp. 7 top (The U.S. Food and Drug Administration), 9 top (Museopedia), 23 bottom (Wellcome Images), 24 bottom (Ballista).

All other images from Shutterstock

Library and Archives Canada Cataloguing in Publication

Rooney, Anne, author
     Biologists in action / Anne Rooney.

(Scientists in action)
Includes index.
Issued in print and electronic formats.
ISBN 978-0-7787-5204-2 (hardcover).--
ISBN 978-0-7787-5208-0 (softcover).--
ISBN 978-1-4271-2156-1 (HTML)

     1. Biologists--Juvenile literature. 2. Biology--Juvenile literature.
I. Title.

QH48.R64 2018   j570   C2018-902999-4
                                  C2018-903000-3

Library of Congress Cataloging-in-Publication Data

Names: Rooney, Anne (Children's author), author.
Title: Biologists in action / Anne Rooney.
Description: New York, New York : Crabtree Publishing, [2019] |
    Series: Scientists in action | Includes index.
Identifiers: LCCN 2018033706 (print) | LCCN 2018038212 (ebook) |
    ISBN 9781427121561 (Electronic) |
    ISBN 9780778752042 (hardcover) |
    ISBN 9780778752080 –(paperback)
Subjects: LCSH: Biologists--Juvenile literature.
Classification: LCC QH309.2 (ebook) | LCC QH309.2 .R66 2019 (print)
    | DDC 646.4/8--dc23
LC record available at https://lccn.loc.gov/2018033706

Crabtree Publishing Company

www.crabtreebooks.com   1-800-387-7650

Printed in the U.S.A./102018/CG20180810

Published in Canada
Crabtree Publishing
616 Welland Ave.
St. Catharines, Ontario
L2M 5V6

Published in the United States
Crabtree Publishing
PMB 59051
350 Fifth Avenue, 59th Floor
New York, New York 10118

Published in the United Kingdom
Crabtree Publishing
Maritime House
Basin Road North, Hove
BN41 1WR

Published in Australia
Crabtree Publishing
3 Charles Street
Coburg North
VIC, 3058

CONTENTS

BIOLOGISTS IN ACTION

In the **rain forest** of Borneo in Southeast Asia, **poachers** illegally trap and kill pangolins. These strange-looking mammals have scales on their bodies that poachers sell for use in traditional Chinese medicine. Biologists keep track of the pangolins' decreasing numbers and help find ways to stop poaching. They are scientists who study living things. Pangolins are also harmed when the forests where they live are cut down. This removes the hollow trees in which they raise their young. Biologists advise foresters on how best to look after the forest **ecosystem**.

What Is a Biologist?

Biologists study organisms—living things of all kinds. This includes plants, animals, and **microorganisms** that can only be seen through a microscope, such as **bacteria**. They work in the field and in laboratories to find out how organisms behave, grow, and function. Biologists also look at whole communities of organisms to see how they interact with each other and their **environment**.

*A biologist holds a three-month-old orphaned pangolin. Without the help of biologists and **conservation** workers, this young animal would die.*

Working with Organisms

Some biologists work with organisms that are grown and bred in laboratories, such as bacteria, fruit flies, or mice. Still other biologists collect plants, fish, insects, or other organisms from the wild. Others observe larger organisms, such as gorillas, trees, or sharks, in their natural settings.

Marine biologists study organisms that live in the seas and oceans.

The work of biologists increases our knowledge of life in all its forms. It leads to advances in medicine when biologists figure out what causes a disease and find new ways to treat it. It helps conservation of animals and plants by protecting environments. By developing hardier and more productive crops and animals, it improves farming and food production. In this book, we will look at how biologists use science practices to guide their investigations and make discoveries in their field.

From the Field: Holly Fearnbach

Holly Fearnbach is a marine biologist who studies on the health of marine mammals, such as dolphins and whales. She uses **drones** to photograph animals and keep track of the weight, health, and pregnancies of individual animals. She examines the bodies of animals that die when they become stranded. She even captures samples of water from whales' **blowholes** to examine the microorganisms that live in their lungs!

A LIFE STUDYING LIFE

The natural world is all around us, even in the heart of the city. There are organisms everywhere; they live in ecosystems that range from the vast oceans to the insides of our own bodies. Biology deals with big, crucial questions that relate to the survival of ourselves and the organisms with which we share the planet. Biologists tackle such questions as:

Biologists often work out in the field, collecting samples and taking measurements.

- How are humans changing ecosystems? How do pollution and **climate change** affect the natural world?

- How quickly are **species** (different types of organisms) dying out? What can we do about this?

- How can we fight diseases that no longer respond to the medicines we use?

- How can we use biology to help farmers and protect our food supply?

- How do modern lifestyles and diet affect our health?

Science seeks to extend our knowledge, and it tries to solve specific problems. For biologists, a question that extends knowledge might be How many species of ants live in this forest?" A question that applies science to a practical problem might be "What causes a disease?"

Big or Small

Some biologists study individual organisms, populations, or ecosystems. Others look at parts of organisms or study processes going on inside organisms, such as the digestion of food. Many biologists do both. **Cells** are the tiny building blocks of living organisms. Working with individual cells, biologists can change the characteristics of an organism and then look at the whole organism to see the effects of the change. For example, a biologist might change a **gene** in a mouse **embryo** to try to protect it against a disease. Then the mouse will be tested after it's born by exposing it to the disease.

These biologists are studying tiny microorganisms that can cause disease in plants.

A biologist working on plant genetics collects seeds.

Biologists at Work

There are many different kinds of biologists. For example, zoologists work with animals, botanists work with plants, ecologists work with whole ecosystems, and microbiologists work with microorganisms. Within these fields, biologists can work in different ways. Some work in biomedicine, looking at how plant or animal bodies use **nutrients** or fight disease. Some use **genetics** to work out how organisms inherit characteristics and change over generations.

STUDYING LIFE THEN AND NOW

The natural world is around us for everyone to see, so it's not surprising that the earliest records of observations are more than 2,000 years old. Early **naturalists** often drew the wrong conclusions as they tried to fit what they saw with what people believed at the time.

*Barnacle geese (above left) nest in Greenland, so for hundreds of years, people in other parts of Europe never saw their nests. They believed the geese grew on trees or driftwood, starting as "goose **barnacles**" (above right) and dropping into the water when fully grown!*

Starting with Science: From Observation to Experiment

Proper scientific investigation of animals and plants began in the 1600s. People started to explore how human and animal bodies work, and discovered in the 1700s how plants photosynthesize. When plants photosynthesize, they use gases from the air, and energy from sunlight, to make food. Scientists began to experiment, trying to find out how the natural world works.

Collecting, Classifying, and Understanding

As long-distance travel became easier, people began to collect and classify organisms, grouping them mostly by their appearance. In 1859, Charles Darwin explained why there are similarities and differences between organisms. His theory of **evolution** shows that animals and plants change over time as they adapt to changing conditions. At around the same time, the Austrian monk Gregor Mendel studied how pea plants inherit characteristics. He found predictable patterns to the way features are inherited.

Detailed models, such as this tiny sea creature in glass, were used to teach biology in the 1800s.

Coming Together

In the 1900s, biologists found out exactly how characteristics are passed from parent to child: Features are stored as information in genes. This discovery lies at the heart of modern biology. The study of how characteristics are inherited is called genetics. It is now used to investigate evolution and to help classify organisms.

Although many questions have been answered in biology, there is much we still don't understand about how organisms function and behave together. There is plenty left for biologists to investigate.

To study and experiment with bacteria, biologists often first grow a colony (group) of the organisms on a plate of agar jelly.

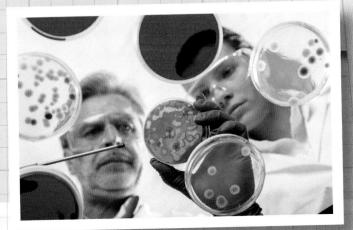

From the Field: Agnes Day

Antibiotics are medicines that act against bacteria. The first antibiotic was discovered in 1928. Their use revolutionized medical treatment, but some bacteria have changed over time, and many antibiotics no longer work. These bacteria are said to be "resistant" to antibiotics. Agnes Day works to find out exactly how bacteria become resistant. She adds genes from resistant bacteria to others that are still killed by antibiotics, and grows them in the lab. She then tests them for resistance. Her work shows how antibiotic resistance might spread between bacteria.

9

INVESTIGATING LIFE

Although scientists in different fields do very different work, they set about their investigations in a similar way. They always begin with a question that they want to answer.

Science Practices

Investigations in science involve the following practices:

- Asking questions
- Developing methods of investigation, including building **models** and designing observations and experiments
- Carrying out investigations
- Analyzing and interpreting data collected
- Using mathematics and technology to process data
- Constructing explanations from evidence
- Communicating findings and conclusions

Step by Step

Scientists design an investigation to answer the question they have set. This involves collecting data. Data can take many forms and can be collected in the lab or the field. For biologists, the data could be the number of bacteria that grow in different conditions or the **migration** path of an animal. It can come from readings, counts, or measurements made by a researcher or from electronic equipment, such as **GPS** tracking.

Scientists process their data to reach conclusions about their original question. The results don't always give a clear answer and often lead to further questions and new research. Sometimes, parts of an investigation have to be repeated, perhaps by changing the method of investigation. Progress is not always straightforward, but scientists are adaptable and resourceful. Sharing results and discussing findings means other scientists can contribute to and benefit from each piece of research.

Biologists can collect data about large mammals by setting up camera traps that will automatically film images of moving animals.

A marine biologist in Florida prepares to examine a captured manatee to collect data about its health and well-being before releasing it again.

All's Fair...

Biologists work with living organisms and have to treat them well. Work with living animals is usually approved by an **ethics** committee that looks carefully at the planned research. Members decide if it is fair and if there is a good reason for doing it, and make sure it does not cause unnecessary suffering to the animals.

From the Field: Bryson Voirin

Bryson Voirin works in the rain forest of Panama in Central America, tracking the sleep patterns of sloths (slow-moving mammals that live all their lives in the trees). He tries to answer the question: Why do sloths sleep more in captivity than in the wild? Voirin uses tiny machines to record patterns of brain activity in sloths in the wild, tracking their sleep. He then compares data from wild sloths and captive sloths to draw conclusions. His research helps scientists understand the function of sleep in other animals, including humans.

Sloths hang upside down in trees and feed on leaves.

ASKING QUESTIONS OF THE WORLD

Biologists might start with a very specific question, such as which gene causes an inherited disease, or a much broader question, such as how noise pollution affects an ecosystem.

Life in the Forest

Forests are the most **biodiverse** habitats in the world and cover nearly a third of all dry land. They are important for many reasons, yet they are under threat. People cut forests down to clear land for building or farming, or to use the wood for fuel or heat. Ecologists who work in forests ask questions about how organisms work together in an ecosystem: What types of animals rely on which plants for a home or food? What role do microorganisms play in a forest? How does human activity affect forest organisms?

Forest ecologists study **habitats** and how they change. They count and track the organisms living there, from microorganisms and insects to plants, birds, and large mammals, and explore how they live and interact.

A medicine to treat high blood pressure is made from the venom (poison) of the deadly lancehead viper that lives in the rain forests of Central America. It is just one of many valuable products that rainforest organisms provide.

How Forests Work

Trees are at the heart of a forest ecosystem, they are what make it a forest. Ecologists study how trees and other plants grow and keep the ecosystem going.

In 1997, biologists in Switzerland were researching how trees use gases from the air. Unexpectedly, they found that trees are connected underground by a network of **fungi** that moves nutrients between them. The discovery has raised many questions: Do trees or fungi start the process of moving chemical food around? Do fungi move chemicals between other plants? As so often happens in science, answering one question has raised many other fascinating questions.

Forest ecosystems are complex. An ecologist checks seeds and berries in a forest to determine the chances of birds successfully breeding and feeding here.

A network of fungal fibers spreads underground through a forest, connecting trees together.

From the Field: Suzanne Simard

Suzanne Simard works on fungi living between tree roots in Canada. She explores the question of how trees "cooperate." Do older trees help younger ones to grow by sharing nutrients? Do trees help each other out when one is in shadow or has lost its leaves? In her experiments, she traces chemicals taken in by the trees' leaves to find out where they end up. She takes samples from the trees and from the fungi between their roots to find out how the chemicals have been used.

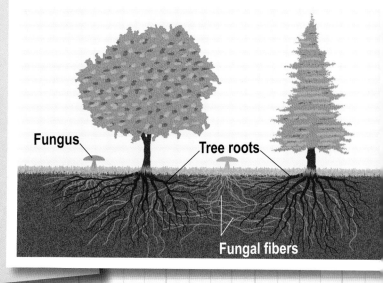

Fungus

Tree roots

Fungal fibers

SEEING BIG AND SMALL

Observation is a powerful tool for biologists. They often collect data by watching, counting, measuring, and recording over time, or by looking in detail at samples, or **specimens**.

Counting and Collecting

Biologists working with small organisms might collect a sample of the environment, such as pond water, or the organisms, such as beetles, to observe in the lab. Biologists working on large organisms, such as trees or lions, observe them in their habitat. They might use cameras, **infrared** sensors, or GPS to track moving animals, or use simpler tools to measure the heights of plants.

Biologists record data carefully and accurately, in a way that will be easy to understand later. They collect as much data as possible, checking and repeating readings or measurements wherever possible. This helps to avoid mistakes and reduces the effect of any single unusual reading or sample, such as an extra-large organism.

Forest ecologists collect data and take photographs in the Australian rain forest.

To track damage to coral reefs in Malaysia, marine biologists take measurements repeatedly over a long period of time.

An International Standard: The Metric System

All biologists use the metric system of measurements. Using the same units makes it very easy for scientists around the world to work together and to share and compare results.

Time after Time

How long data collection takes depends on the question. Insects breed quickly and live a short time, so data about an insect's life cycle can be collected in a short time. Sometimes, data collection takes decades. A study of the changing populations of animals in a forest will need data collected over many years.

Starting from Scratch

All wildlife on the Indonesian island of Krakatau was killed by a volcanic eruption in 1883. Soon after, scientists asked: How does a forest ecosystem become established and grow over time? Biologists have been visiting the island since the 1880s to answer the question. They survey plants and animals and try to work out how they arrived on the island. For example, were they blown there by the wind, carried by the tide, or introduced by visiting birds or humans?

A new, small volcano growing on the island of Krakatau erupts, belching gases into the island's ecosystem.

TRYING THINGS OUT

Biologists can carry out experiments in the field or the lab, but it's easier to control conditions in the lab. Experiments in the field can be disrupted by weather, the unpredictable behavior of other organisms, and other factors. In the lab, biologists can change one feature of the environment at a time to see what effect the change has. For example, a biologist can compare plants grown in the same type of soil, with the same amount of water and light, and change just the temperature.

Small plants can easily be grown in a laboratory for experimentation.

From the Field: Darío Vázquez-Albacete

Darío Vázquez-Albacete, originally from Spain, works in Denmark changing bacteria so that they produce useful chemicals. He adds genes from plants, which make **enzymes** of a type called P540. Plants use P540 to make chemicals that protect them against attack by plant-eaters, insects, and microorganisms. Vázquez-Albacete is hoping to turn bacteria into miniature factories that can use the P540 to churn out chemicals for use in cancer treatments.

A forest ecologist uses a hand-held scanner to examine a coconut crab. The biologist disturbs the animal as little as possible during the investigation.

Wild Experiments

Experiments in the field are more realistic because the conditions are closer to how an organism actually lives. A forest ecologist can only test whether an endangered animal can survive in a different type of forest by putting it in the new environment and tracking its progress. Many experiments that start in the lab are followed by field trials, during which a technique, product, or organism is tested in the natural environment. For example, a treatment developed in the lab to protect pine trees from disease must eventually be tested on trees in a pine forest.

Experiments in Genetics

Biologists use genetics to work out how organisms function, or to change their characteristics. Biologists can experiment with removing or adding genes to work out what a particular gene does. Then they can use that information to produce altered organisms. For example, finding a gene that allows a plant to survive with little water helps scientists develop crops to grow in dry areas. Finding a gene that causes a disease can help scientists to develop treatments.

The work of geneticists involves a lot of time in the lab using special equipment.

FROM FIELD TO LAB

Biologists go on field trips to observe organisms in their habitat and gather data. Sometimes, they make field trips to collect organisms for investigation.

Blood, Sweat, and Tears

Conditions in the field can be extreme, uncomfortable, and even dangerous. Biologists often need to travel by plane, helicopter, or boat, or trek long distances on foot, to get to the places they study, such as deep in the rain forest. Some biologists work on mountaintops, in caves, up trees, or underwater.

Biologists brave difficult conditions to search for tiny scorpions just millimeters long in a cave system in Portugal.

Forest ecologists might need to carry heavy or delicate equipment, such as video cameras or materials to make a treetop observation platform. In the forest, they may have to wait a long time to spot animals or track them over long distances to gather the data they need. They sometimes carry chemicals, such as medicines, which have to be kept cool, and samples or organisms that must be kept safe. They might also need to contend with leeches, biting insects, poisonous snakes, heat, humidity, or cold.

In the Lab

Data collection in the lab takes many forms. Biologists might carry out experiments to produce data. They might observe the behavior of small organisms, **dissect** organisms, or use microscopes to examine parts of organisms in detail. They may also conduct chemical tests. Lab work is often a follow-up to fieldwork. Even a forest ecologist working on giant trees will take samples of bark, soil, leaves, and insects to work with in the lab.

Biologists use microscopes of different types to examine their samples.

FACTS FROM FINDINGS

Biologists need to process and interpret the data they collect to yield useful information. This can involve calculations, computer modeling, comparison with other data, and searching for patterns in the data. The results are used to offer an answer to the original question or to explain something.

(above) Data collected in forests can be processed later to answer ecologists' questions.

(right) A biologist uses a computer to analyze the data collected from tracked mountain cats in South America.

Working with Data

A team of forest ecologists led by Manuel Guariguata in Peru observed how land that had been cleared, farmed, and then abandoned slowly returned to forest. They wanted to find out whether the regrown forest had greater **biodiversity** if it grew naturally or was artificially planted. They counted the different types of organisms found in the natural forest over a period of time, and in another area that was part of a tree-planting program.

Data are just a starting point. The scientists needed to find meaningful patterns or trends in the data that they collected. When processing their data, they compared the number and types of different organisms found in both areas and compared levels of disease and attack by pests in each. Comparing the data led them to useful conclusions. The naturally reforested land had greater biodiversity and resisted disease and pest damage better than the managed forest.

From the Field: Janelle Ayres

Janelle Ayres works at the Salk Institute in La Jolla, California, studying the body's response to illness. Beginning with the question "How does suppressed appetite (wanting to eat less) affect the progress of illness in sick mice?" she infected mice with salmonella bacteria to make them ill. Some were fed more, while others ate as little as they wanted. Mice that ate more survived longer.

The data collected included a count of bacteria in different parts of the body. This revealed that bacteria stayed in the gut of feeding mice but spread through the bodies of those that didn't eat. From the data, Ayres concluded that bacteria spread if there are not enough nutrients from food for them in the gut, causing more-severe illness. Further research could show whether this happens in humans, too, and give us a clue about how to control infections.

Mice and rats are used to explore many questions in biological investigations.

SHARING FINDINGS

Science is most useful when findings are shared with other scientists and the public. Within the scientific community, results feed into other projects and spark new investigations. Sharing with the public can change how people behave—making healthier lifestyle choices, for example—or lead to new products, such as medicines.

In the Public Eye

Biologists present and discuss their work at conferences, as well as write books and articles for scientific **journals**. They give full details of their methods and results, inviting other experts to check and add to their work.

Some biologists appear at science festivals, give public lectures at museums, or appear on TV or radio to describe their findings to the public. They post videos and articles online and explain their work in newspapers and magazines. Work on popular subjects, such as treatments for common diseases, forest conservation, or work on large animals, like elephants or pandas, attracts a lot of public attention.

A fish biologist presents her findings to other scientists at a conference.

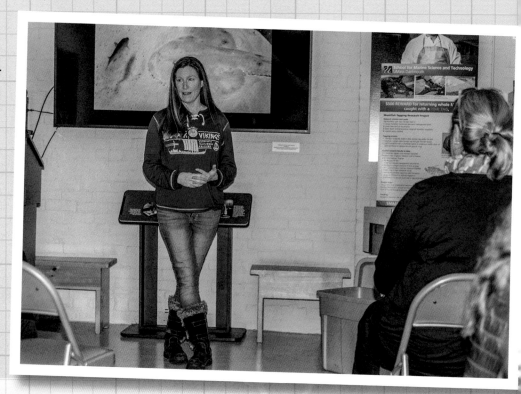

From Climate to Insects and Back Again

Rupert Seidl works with a team in Vienna, Austria, that includes experts on forest ecology and climate change. The team studies the impact of climate change on pests damaging European forests. As the climate warms, new types of insect pests can move into Europe from elsewhere and damage trees. Seidl's results found that damage to forest trees caused by these pests makes it harder for trees to take carbon dioxide from the atmosphere. That, in turn, leaves more carbon dioxide in the air, making global warming worse. The warmer climate favors the insect pests, and so the cycle continues. His team's research has shown other scientists that slowing the movement of new insect pests into European forests will help in the fight against climate change.

Insect pests can devastate a forest in a short period of time.

The Human Genome Project

Sharing research allows other scientists to build on the findings of an investigation, taking the work in new directions. The results of a project mapping the human genome (listing all the genes that define the human body) were made freely available throughout the world. This has led, as intended, to the development of new ideas for treating diseases and inherited conditions. It has also led to discoveries about how some genes are distributed in the human population.

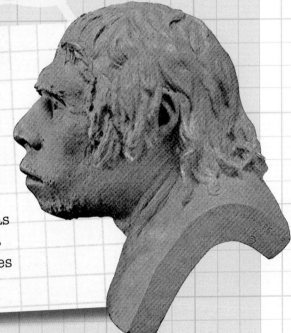

Studying the genome of a type of early humans, called Neanderthals, reveals that modern people have kept around 2 percent of the Neanderthal genome.

A WHOLE LIVING WORLD

Science is rarely carried out just by individuals. Most modern biologists work in large teams and often collaborate with scientists in other countries. Everyone benefits from a wider pool of expertise, with people bringing different ideas and points of view to a project.

Working Together

Biologists with different specialties may work together, or biologists might work with other types of scientists on a project. Biologists who know about the bodies of modern animals often work with **paleontologists** to work out how organisms in the past lived and behaved. Ecologists working on forest ecosystems might work closely with other biologists, as well as scientists who understand water systems, the soil, and rocks.

(above) Biologists and environmental scientists work together to discuss water quality and the prospects for endangered fish in California.

(left) Biologists and fossil experts figure out the colors of long-dead animals, such as this archaeopteryx, by comparing fossilized feathers with the feathers of modern birds.

Peer-to-Peer

Biologists have their work peer-reviewed, or checked by other experts, to make sure it is as accurate and reliable as possible before it is accepted as fact. Other scientists often make valuable suggestions about the design of a study, the methods used, how the data have been processed, and whether the conclusions are valid and sound.

The SAFE Project

SAFE (Stability of Altered Forest Ecosystems) employs 400 researchers from 16 countries to study how human activities affect forest ecosystems in Southeast Asia. They work with the logging industry to minimize the effects of change on the forest. Forests that were once heavily logged will be replaced with forests managed for farming. The aim is to combine farming with conservation.

The scientists working together include many biologists and biodiversity experts, but also scientists working on water systems and the atmosphere. Biologists on the SAFE Project work with birds, bats, small and large mammals, insects, amphibians, and plant life. The results of their studies are already changing practices in the region and elsewhere, including forests in West Africa and South America.

Biologists on the SAFE Project aim to protect biodiveristy in areas where forest is destroyed to make way for farming.

A GROWING FIELD

New areas in biology open up all the time as knowledge and technology advance. For example, biologists can now use picture-based phone apps to track animals in the wild. They can log evidence such as footprints, droppings, or sightings, which is then immediately added to a database. Changing threats to the natural world bring up new questions, too: How can we tackle tiny pieces of plastic being eaten by animals and eventually turning up in the food we eat? How can we fight new diseases? Answering one question often opens up new areas for research. Finding out about the wide variety of microorganisms that live in our bodies has led to research into how health, nutrition, and disease are affected by our **microbiome**.

Wildlife parks are fun to visit, and you can also learn about the work of wildlife biologists and conservationists.

Some citizen-science projects encourage you to get out into the landscape and spot and record the organisms that live around you.

Get Involved

It's never too early to develop an interest in biological research. You can join a science club, visit local museums and open days at labs or hospitals, hear talks and see demonstrations at science fairs, or volunteer to take part in surveys. Many science institutes and charities run projects in which the public take part. There are also many "citizen-science" projects that invite people to process data from real investigations. For example, you could watch footage of chimpanzees in the jungle and mark particular types of behavior, or count penguins in Antarctica!

PROJECT: KEEPING CLEAN

Try your own investigation in biology. You probably can't visit the rain forest, but you can investigate the microbes, or microorganisms, that turn up on your own body.

Ask a Question

Think of questions you can ask about cleanliness and protecting ourselves from harmful microbes. Where do microbes come from? How can we stop them from getting into our bodies? When do microbes grow most quickly?

Dirty hands are home to millions of microorganisms.

Investigate!

You're always told to wash your hands—but how effective is it as a way of getting rid of bacteria? Let's find out. You will need the following equipment:

- Five disposable plastic boxes with clear lids, such as takeout food containers

- Plastic wrap

- A marker pen and ruler

- Agar flakes (unflavored vegetarian jelly)

- A measuring jug and spoon

- Soap

- Antibacterial gel or wipes.

You will investigate how effectively plain water, soap, and antibacterial gel or wipes remove microbes from your skin.

A dish of agar jelly provides nourishment for growing bacteria.

Follow These Steps to Carry Out Your Investigation

1 With adult help, make up 16 ounces (0.5 liters) of agar jelly, following the instructions on the packet.

2 Wash five clear boxes and lids. Pour 0.5 inches (1.25 cm) agar jelly into each box. Cover with film and leave the jelly to set.

3 Use the marker pen and ruler to draw a grid on each lid, with squares of 0.5 inches (1.25 cm). Put the lids on the boxes.

4 Expose one box to the air for 10 seconds and then put the lid on. This is your **control**: You have not touched it to introduce any bacteria.

5 Now get your hands dirty in some way. You could stroke a pet, do a bit of gardening, run them over a dirty surface outside, or just rub them in your hair.

6 Holding your fingers together, press a dirtied hand lightly against the agar in the second box for 10 seconds. Put the lid back on and label the box.

7 Wash your hands thoroughly, and then dirty them again in the same way. This time, rinse them in hot water and place a hand on the agar in the next box for 10 seconds. Close the box and label it.

8 Repeat the process, once using soap and hot water to clean your hands and once using antibacterial gel or wipes.

9 Leave the boxes undisturbed for two or three days. They must all be at the same temperature and in the same amount of light to make a fair test.

10 Look through the lids. Can you see anything growing on the jelly? The bacteria from your hands feed on the jelly, then grow and reproduce. Use the marker pen to outline on the lid the areas covered by bacteria in each box.

11 Count the number of squares on the lid that are more than half-covered by any outlined areas.

12 Draw up a table showing how many squares are filled for each box:

Box	Number of squares with bacteria
Untouched (control)	
Unwashed hands	
Rinsed with hot water	
Washed with soap and warm water	
Cleaned with gel	

When you have finished with the boxes, throw them away without opening them.

From Data to Results

Now you need to work out what you have found out. Which box had most bacteria, and which had the least? What conclusions can you draw from your evidence? How can you clean your hands most effectively?

It would be good to communicate your conclusion and explanation to others, as this is useful information to share. Can you find an interesting way to present your findings, such as making a poster or a video? How could you extend your investigation to work out which conditions favor the growth of bacteria?

LEARNING MORE

BOOKS

Cornell, Kari. *Urban Biologist Danielle Lee*. Lerner Publications, 2016.

Koonz, Robin, *Marine Biologists* (Scientists in the Field). Rourke Publishing, 2015.

Mangal, Mélina. *The Vast Wonder of the World: Biologist Ernest Everett Just*. Millbrook Press, 2018.

Montgomery, Sy. *The Hyena Scientist* (Scientists in the Field). HMH Books for Young Readers, 2018.

Owen, Ruth. *Marine Biologists* (Out of the Lab: Extreme Jobs in Science). Powerkids Press, 2013.

Payment, Simone. *Biologists at Work* (Scientists at Work). Britannica Educational Publishing, 2017.

Valice, Kim Perez. *The Orca Scientists* (Scientists in the Field). HMH Books for Young Readers, 2018.

PLACES TO VISIT

Many large cities have a natural history museum, a botanical garden, or a zoo. As well as exhibitions of plants and animals, these often have displays or information about the work of zoologists, botanists, and other biologists.

If you are near the coast, you might be able to visit an aquarium or sea-life center; inland there might be a wildlife park nearby. Many of these carry out work in conservation and other areas of biology.

Universities and colleges with biology departments frequently host public science fairs and festivals where you can find out about the work of biologists and learn about their research projects.

Some large research facilities, such as the Salk Institute in California, open part of their buildings to the public and organize tours and talks.

ONLINE

These websites offer the chance to be involved in a range of citizen-science projects, including many in biology:

www.nationalgeographic.org/idea/citizen-science-projects/

http://blogs.plos.org/citizensci/2017/01/06/top-10-citizen-science-projects-of-2016-from-microbes-to-meteors/

www.zooniverse.org/

http://content.yardmap.org/
Take part in a project to provide, track, and protect habitats for wildlife in North America.

www.environmentalscience.org/career/biologist
Find out what it takes to become a biologist and what biologists do.

#iamabiologist
Use this hashtag on Twitter to find biologists you can follow and learn about their work.

GLOSSARY

bacteria Microorganisms with a single cell, some of which cause diseases

barnacle Small crustacean that often lives on rocks, driftwood, or structures submerged in the ocean

biodiverse/biodiversity The variety of organisms that live in an environment

blowhole The hole at the top of a whale's head through which it breathes air

cell Building block of living organisms; all organisms are made up of one or more cells, often of different types (such as blood, bone, and muscle cells)

climate change Alteration in long-term weather patterns

conservation The attempt to keep alive organisms that are in danger of dying out and to protect environments from damage

control An object, individual, or group that is not changed or processed in any way in an experiment; used to make sure that any effects seen in other objects, individuals, or groups have come about as a result of deliberately changing conditions in the experiment

dissect To cut up carefully in order to look at the structure of an organism

drone A small, robotic flying vehicle that is controlled remotely and is often fitted with cameras or other equipment

ecosystem An environment and all the organisms that live in it

embryo An organism in the early stages of development, before it is born or hatches from an egg

environment A place where organisms live, with its particular physical structures, atmosphere, and water supply; can be natural, such as a forest, or human-made, such as a city

enzyme A chemical that makes particular chemical reactions proceed more quickly or easily but is not itself permanently changed in the reaction

ethics The branch of philosophy that deals with ideas of right and wrong

evolution The process by which organisms change over time to adapt to changes in their environment; organisms that adapt to suit their environment better are most likely to survive and breed

fungi Organisms that are neither plants nor animals, including mushrooms, yeasts, and molds

gene A segment of the chemical DNA that holds a chemical "code" defining a single characteristic of an organism

genetics The study of how characteristics pass from one generation of organisms to the next, which genes produce which characteristics, and how they work to make organisms the way they are

GPS The Global Positioning System that uses satellites going around Earth to track objects or organisms from place to place

habitat The environment in which a particular organism lives

infrared Invisible radiation (energy waves) that we experience as heat; infrared cameras can detect animals in the dark, because the heat from warm-blooded animals stands out against cooler surroundings

journal A publication that presents articles written by experts on scientific or other academic topics

marine biologist A biologist who specializes in the ocean ecosystem and organisms that live in the sea

microbiome The collection of microorganisms that live in the human body. In our body, we have more microorganisms than human cells

microorganism A living organism too small to see without a microscope

migration Movement of an animal following a set path at a particular time of year, usually to move to new feeding grounds or avoid bad weather

model An object or image that is used to show or explain an idea

naturalist A person who studies nature, especially plants or animals

nutrient A chemical an organism needs and which it gets from its food (or the soil, in the case of a plant)

paleontologist A scientist who studies fossils

poacher A person who traps or kills animals illegally

rain forest Tropical jungle characterized by very dense plant growth and a wide variety of wildlife

specimen An individual plant or animal, or a sample of something produced by an organism (such as blood or seeds)

species A genetically distinct type of organism, such as a leopard or an oak tree; organisms of different species cannot generally breed together

INDEX

ABOUT THE AUTHOR

Anne Rooney is a full-time writer, specializing in books on science and technology, and the history of science, for young people and adults. Her main interests are evolution and other aspects of the biological sciences, and she writes frequently on these topics. In 2018, she was shortlisted for the Royal Society Young Person's Book Prize.